FIGHTING STATESMAN:
Sen. George Norris

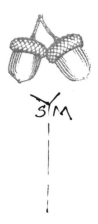

3YM

Fighting Statesman: Sen. George Norris is part of THE
REAT HEARTLANDERS SERIES. This collection of
ographies for children describes the lives of local heroes
men and women of all races and careers – who have
ade a lasting contribution to the nation and the world.

FIGHTING STATESMAN:
Sen. George Norris

Copyright © 2001 by Acorn Books

Acorn Books
7337 Terrace
Kansas City, MO 64114

Cataloguing-in-Publication Data
Christine Pappas and J.L. Wilkerson
    Fighting Statesman: Sen. George Norris / by Christine
Pappas and J.L. Wilkerson
    Library of Congress Control Number: 00-134847
    Series Title: The Great Heartlanders Series
ISBN 0-9664470-5-0
1. George Norris, 1861-1944 - Juvenile literature. 2. Ne-
braska - Biography - History - United States Senate -
Midwest.

10 9 8 7 6 5 4 3 2 1

Dedication

For all the friends and supporters of THE GREAT HEARTLANDERS SERIES who understand the importance of providing children the opportunity to learn about their local heroes.

Christine Pappas dedicates her contribution to *Fighting Statesman: Sen. George Norris* to "My Niece, Jana (Banana)."

Acknowledgements

Linda Hein, Curator of the Norris Home and Museum in McCook, Nebraska.
The staff of the Jane Pope Geske Heritage Room of Nebraska Authors at Bennett Martin Public Library in Lincoln, Nebraska.
Betty Dixon, John Parkison and Nettye Hugh Jones for their careful attention to detail.

Book production by Acorn Books, Kansas City, Missouri.
Cover image: Norris Dam on Clinch River in Tennessee; insert, George Norris.

Photo Credits:
Nebraska State Historical Society: cover (Norris inset) and pages 4, 14, 18, 30, 46 and 106.
United States National Archives and Records Administration: cover (Norris Dam) and pages 86, 94, 96, 98 and 104.
Library of Congress: pages 56 and 92.

Contents

❧ *1* ❧

The Lesson of the Tree

George Norris tied the reins to the plow's handles. He unharnessed the horses and led them to a stream running beside the field. The spring afternoon in northern Ohio was unusually hot. George was glad the plowing was done for the day.

From the nearby orchard, his mother called. George grabbed a water jug and headed across the stream and into the orchard.

Mary Norris stood beside a tiny tree. She asked George to hold the sapling upright while she set it in the hole she'd dug. She wanted to shovel dirt evenly around the tender roots.

1

George bent down. His back and arms ached from the hours he'd spent plowing the field. Even his hands hurt from gripping the plow handles all day.

George was ten years old and worked as hard as any man. His older brother, John Henry, died seven years ago in the Civil War and his father died six months later of pneumonia. Since then George, his six sisters and mother ran the farm.

George looked up at his mother. That morning, when it was too early to go into the orchard, Mary worked at her spinning wheel. By winter she would have spun the thread, woven the cloth and made clothes for all of her oldest children. (The little children wore hand-me-downs.) In the afternoon sun, the sweat dripped from Mary's nose and forehead. Her hands, callused and red, were caked in mud. Mary was as exhausted as her son.

George didn't resent working so hard. By fall corn, potatoes, carrots, peaches, cherries and apples would fill the cellar. By Thanksgiving rabbits, pheasants and deer would hang in the smokehouse. George, an excellent marksman, could shoot as well as any man. How could he resent work that was so productive?

And yet he wondered at his mother's laboring over this tiny tree. The family's orchard had dozens of healthy trees.

Years later in his autobiography, George said he watched his mother pack the dirt firmly over the planted sapling, and he asked her, "Why do you work so hard, mother? We now have more fruit than we can possibly use. You'll be dead long before this tree comes to bearing."

Mary Norris took a drink from the jug of water and then poured the rest around the tiny tree.

"I may never see this tree in bearing," she said, "but somebody will."

"That was the unselfishness of the pioneer era," George wrote later.

His father had built a farm that continued to sustain his family even after his death. His mother carried on that pioneer tradition. Work, she believed, wasn't only meant to answer an immediate need, but also to provide for a future need.

For the rest of his life, George measured his own achievements against that simple guidepost. Sometimes he succeeded. And sometimes he didn't.

George's father died of pneumonia when the boy was three and a half years old. Mary, who was pregnant at the time, and her children remained on the farm.

In his autobiography, George wrote, "There on that farm I lost all fear of poverty. I learned to live most simply, and I learned to get a great joy out of work....I grew up to believe wholly and completely in men and women who lived simply, frugally, and in fine faith....

"Unconsciously there developed in that pioneer Ohio region a great respect for justice and a great sympathy for the oppressed. As a boy I saw with my own eyes the struggles of a democracy where the first problem is not protection of the strong and the powerful but instead encouragement and inspiration for the weak and the unfortunate. In the organization of the life of this democracy, and in the development of its conceptions of social justice, it has seemed to me, is the spirit of America."

2

Remarkable Boy

The meeting hall in Clyde, Ohio, was impressive. For a country teenager like George, the hall's carpeted floor, brass lamps and carved desks seemed lavish.

George looked across the hall at the men sitting on a long, wooden bench. They wore white shirts and fine black suits. The neatly groomed men were all doctors and lawyers from Clyde. They were the "Sons of Thunder," the best-educated debate team that George and his friends had ever faced.

George glanced at the young men and farmers who stood next to him. They had walked the three miles to Clyde after finishing their day's work. Dressed in homemade shirts and high-top boots, George and his friends looked like country bumpkins. And, as if to drive the point home, they called themselves the "Mud Stompers."

During the mid and late 1800s, debate societies

were popular. From big cities in the east to tiny towns on the prairie, citizens met regularly for debates about politics, philosophy, the arts and other subjects. In these formal contests two teams argued with each other in order to defend or attack a given resolution. The highly organized discussions sprang from colonial days when people came together for Town Hall meetings.

The Mud Stompers certainly weren't new to debating competitions. They met weekly, and once a month debated other local teams, mostly farmers like themselves.

Good debaters had to think fast on their feet. They had to defend or attack whatever resolution was presented. And so they needed a broad knowledge of history, politics, science, art and religion. Just in the last three months, the Stompers had argued a variety of resolutions:

Resolved: That water is more destructive than fire.
Resolved: That Ulysses S. Grant was a greater general than Robert E. Lee.
Resolved: That a human is a free moral agent.

George had never found anything he enjoyed more than debating. Debating was a game for the mind. And George enjoyed games – contests of any kind. He even liked corn husking bees. George spent hours practicing in cornfields throughout the county. He had his own husking tool. With the sharp-pointed hook fastened to his hand by a leather strap, he ripped off the tough husks from ears of corn. He was one of the fastest cornhuskers in the county. George approached debate contests with the same competitive spirit as he did corn-husking.

At the Clyde Town Hall, the resolution was announced:

Resolved: That any person who fought for or supported the Confederacy during the Civil War should be forever denied the right to vote in local, state and national elections.

Abraham Lincoln's death and the end of the Civil War had occurred almost a dozen years earlier. The struggles of Reconstruction, a plan to rebuild the nation after the war, dragged on year after year. One of the Reconstruction laws denied southern sympathizers the right to vote. People held strong and differing opinions about this issue. But good debaters could argue for or against any resolution brought up for discussion.

One of the judges tossed a coin to determine which team – the Sons or the Stompers – would argue for the resolution and which against. George's team won the toss. They chose to argue against the resolution.

A member of the Sons' team spoke first. He said that taking up arms against one's country, as Confederate soldiers had done, was the act of a traitor. Traitors had no civil rights, certainly not the right to vote. He said a traitor should not be allowed to participate in a government that he had tried to overthrow.

The first debater for the Stompers said that citizens were tired of regional conflicts. The nation could never find real peace until everyone – northern whites, blacks and southern whites – shared an equal citizenship under the law.

When George's turn came to argue against the resolution, he said that any law denying full citizenship to one group always caused resentments to grow between people. He pointed to the ill treatment of Catholics in Great Britain and the slave conditions of serfs in Russia. And then he quoted the U.S. Constitution and its promise of life, liberty and the pursuit of happiness.

George's team won the debate. The Mud
Stompers had presented the most convincing argu-
ments on the resolution. Afterwards several
Stompers debaters told George that his rebuttal
was excellent, and that he had handled himself with
exceptional skill. Two of the lawyers from Clyde
congratulated George. They said his knowledge of
the constitution was remarkable for one so young.

George felt very proud after such praise. All the
way home, George repeated the flattering words in
his head. "Excellent." "Exceptional skill." "Remarkable." He imagined himself being carried aloft on
the shoulders of the Mud Stompers. He imagined
his name in the local paper, his name on the lips of
people all over northern Ohio. The team's excellent
debater. A remarkable boy. Was there a greater
honor in the entire world than public glory?

George was born and grew up in northern Ohio. After graduating from Northern Indiana Normal School (later Valparaiso University) in 1880, George lived in Washington Territory for a short time.

3

Baldwin University

The next September, sixteen-year-old George set out for college. Baldwin University was in Berea, a town on the outskirts of Cleveland. George's two sisters, Emma and Clara, also enrolled in the school. Despite her own lack of a formal education, Mary Norris actively encouraged the schooling of all her children.

George needed little encouragement. As he later wrote, he was "ambitious and hungry for education." What George needed was money. Besides working at the Norris farm, he hired on at neighboring farms. Even so, funds were always scarce.

Thrift was essential. There was no money for entertainment or frills. Few children in rural Ohio could afford a college education, but the Norrises were determined to make the necessary sacrifices. George wore the same suit of clothes every day. When the suit became ragged his sisters mended it.

11

Mary dreamed of traveling to Georgia where her son, John Henry, was buried. She worried that his grave was unattended and unmarked. But there was no money for a trip to the south.

Luckily the college tuition was low. Its founder, John Baldwin, wanted a school where poor young men and women could work and learn simultaneously.

George and his sisters rented the second floor of a house. Their three rooms included two small bedrooms connected by a large room that served as the kitchen, dining room and living room.

Chores were shared. George chopped wood in the backyard and carried the kindling and the water upstairs. Emma and Clara cooked, mended and cleaned. Laundry was divided: the sisters scrubbed and rinsed, and George hung the wash on a line in the yard.

George studied Latin, Greek, German, French, algebra, natural science, history, English grammar, physiology and botany. By the end of the year, he received a perfect 10 for seven courses, and 9.85, 9.8 and 9.0 for the remaining three. When not studying, George participated on the debate team.

Outstanding grades. Hard work. Wise economy. It is the portrait of a remarkable boy – an incomplete portrait, however.

One night George and several of his friends climbed to the top of the college's bell tower. Earlier that day, construction workers, repairing the chapel, had left wooden boards on the roof. "This gang of night raiders," George later wrote, planned to toss the boards to the ground and start a bonfire. The long, unwieldy boards tumbled through the air, sometimes bouncing against the chapel walls. They hit the ground in a splintering clatter, which only added to prankish fun.

After the last board sailed off the tower, George and the others climbed to the ground. To their horror they saw that the falling boards had shattered the glass in several large chapel windows.

Someone whispered, "Let's get out of here."

The next instant everyone scattered.

Later that night, George lay sleepless in bed. What should he do? The thought of turning himself in caused his stomach to tighten into a knot. George's small savings couldn't begin to pay for the damaged windows. Would the school expel him? What would Mary say?

George and his sisters, Emma and Clara, rented the second floor of a house. The three rooms included two small bedrooms connected by a large room that served as the kitchen, dining room and living room. Thrift was essential. There was no money for entertainment or frills.

George later wrote, "Both sisters were very attractive, and the closeness of the quarters embarrassed me because when men students called upon them there was no place where I could go except that tiny bedroom."

(This photograph of George and his sisters was taken several years before they went away to school.)

❈ 4 ❈

Honorable Boys

The next day everyone at the school gathered outside the chapel to see the broken windows. George was there, too.

The school's janitor handed something to Dr. Aaron Schuyler, Baldwin's president, and then nodded to a boy named P.P. Hardy. Hardy, who stood next to George, was one of the boys on the roof last night.

George held his breath.

Dr. Schuyler held up a black button.

"I believe you're missing something," he said to Hardy.

Hardy felt the back of his coat. One of the two buttons on his belt was missing. Earlier that morning the janitor had found the missing button under one of the broken windows. When the students gathered outside the chapel, he spotted Hardy's coat with only one button – an exact match for the lost button.

"I don't believe you did this by yourself," Schuyler said to Hardy.

The boy admitted he'd tossed the boards from the roof. Hardy apologized. Schuyler asked for the names of the other culprits, but Hardy wouldn't tell. Schuyler persisted. Hardy buried his hands in his pockets, but George could see that he was shaking with fear. Schuyler demanded to know the names. The boy remained silent. Finally he apologized again, but he refused to name the other boys.

For a second night George didn't sleep. He thought about Hardy. But for some reason a strange image began entering his mind. It was the image of a grave. A hand moved across the headstone, as if trying to discover the fading inscription.

One at a time the letters revealed themselves —
J O H N H E N R Y. George's brother, buried
somewhere in a faraway land.

He died of a bullet wound shortly before Gen.
William Sherman's army reached Atlanta. Mary
Norris had begged her son not to join the army, and
he promised he wouldn't. But when all his friends
enlisted, John Henry could no longer remain behind. Mary had pleaded. He told his mother he
couldn't let his friends fight his battles for him.
Now he was buried somewhere in Georgia.

John Henry had believed in something so
fiercely that he gave his life for it. He fought and
died for his country. Now he lay in an unmarked
grave. Someone passing by would never realize the
terrible price the young Ohioan had paid for his
belief.

George waited 60 years to tell the story of the
bell tower. Hardy never told the names. He pro-
tected his friends. And none of those friends
stepped forward to thank him. They were too afraid
of detection. Hardy alone took the punishment.

For the rest of his life, George carried in his
heart these two stories.

Two acts of honor — with no public glory.

At Northern Indiana Normal School (Valparaiso), George met nine students who did everything together and shared an interest in debate. They called themselves the L.U.N. Some people believed L.U.N. stood for "Loyal United Nine." However, after the friends tried to get George elected president of the Crescent Literary Society, the group became known as "Lunatics Under Norris." George lost the election, but his L.U.N. friends were George's closest throughout his life. They met every summer until 1943 at a cabin in Michigan (shown here) that George built with his own hands.

❧ 5 ❧

Washington Territory

George waited nervously at the St. Paul, Minnesota, train depot. Everything he owned was in a small leather bag that once belonged to his father. In his hand was a ticket for Walla Walla, Washington.

George attended Baldwin for one year and then went on to Northern Indiana Normal School (later Valparaiso University). His school years were a three-part pattern: learn, farm, teach. George attended classes until he ran out of money, and then he found work – farming in the summer and teaching in the winter.

George earned a law degree from Northern Indiana, but after graduation he couldn't find a job. He taught school instead.

Around that time recruiting companies sent agents throughout Ohio, trying to talk people into moving west. Great job and land opportunities in

Washington Territory, one of the recruiters told Mary and George. And so the two talked it over and decided that George should go to Washington and start a law business. If the country proved as attractive as the recruiters said, Mary would follow.

The train out of St. Paul was crowded with immigrants. Most were prospectors and miners who spoke little English. Experienced travelers, they carried lightweight luggage and blankets to sleep on at night. The train cars had no seats, only wooden benches along the walls. There wasn't a dining car either. The train stopped often and peddlers sold food to the passengers, mostly bologna, cheese and crackers.

When George arrived in Walla Walla, he discovered that the country was nothing like the recruiting agent described.

In his autobiography, George later described his impressions. "It was dusty, and dirty, and desolate, and uninviting. It was no place for my mother. My money was running low. I tried vainly in every way to procure work of some kind, suffering failure after failure. I was becoming worried and desperate."

Finally George found work as a teacher in a country school about 15 miles north of Walla Walla. Again he boarded a train, arriving in Bolles Junction during the night.

He stepped onto the dark, empty platform and watched the train disappear into the night. Off in the distance he saw a light. A farm house, he hoped. He had instructions to find the farmhouse of a family named Lee. By the time he arrived at the front door, he had fallen twice in the dark, cutting and bruising his face and hands.

The Lees' house was small. The farmer, his wife and three children lived in three rooms. That night George slept on their floor. The next day Lee introduced him to the families in the district. None of them offered to rent the newcomer a room. And so George ended up living in a railroad shed. Sunlight, and later snow, streamed in through the loosely boarded walls and roof.

The hastily constructed schoolhouse, built of

warped green lumber, was also drafty. George later recalled that woodpeckers and other birds often flew through the schoolroom.

By the end of the school term, George and Mr. Lee had become friends. They often went fishing and hunting together. Lee was surprised that schoolteacher George was such a crack shot.

One day the two men traveled across Washington to a new town called Dayton, north of Olympia. Lee thought George might find work as a lawyer there. The main building in Dayton was a brewery. Lee and George went inside to buy a beer.

The place was full of loggers. George later described the leader of the men: "a huge man, well over six feet, with powerful shoulders, a hairy chest exposed by his rough shirt open at the neck, a heavy growth of whiskers, and a great mop of hair. This boss was intrigued when he learned I was a schoolteacher, and apparently sensed some fun for his men…He was determined that I join them every time they ordered a round of drinks."

When George refused the drinks, the logging boss became angry. He backed George up against the bar and threatened to pour beer down his throat. Loggers surrounded George, completely boxing him in.

Something inside George exploded. For the last twelve months, he felt like a man adrift. It was a year of one disappointment after another. He had left Ohio with grand dreams of coming to Washington to practice law. And now here he stood in a dirty bar, staring into the face of a bully.

George reached in his pocket and felt the handle of his gun. He warned the big man that if he didn't step aside he'd shoot him.

Lee, who was at the opposite end of the bar, saw the commotion and pushed his way through the crowd.

"For God's sake," he said to the boss, "leave him alone! He's a dead shot, and he'll kill you."

After a moment, the loggers and their boss backed away. The fight was over.

George wrote what happened next.

"I had had enough of Washington Territory. Whatever thoughts I may have had of establishing a law practice there died that afternoon in the brewery. At the end of the week, with the funds I had accumulated, I bought a ticket east for Nebraska."

Nebraska

When Mary Norris realized she and George wouldn't be living in Washington Territory, she bought 80 acres in Nebraska. One of her daughters, George's sister Effie, lived in the state. Like his mother, George had high hopes that his future was in the American west. To encourage him, Mary gave George the deed to the Nebraska land.

A few months later, George and another lawyer, a friend from Northern Indiana, opened a law office in Beatrice, Nebraska. Using the money he'd earned teaching and a loan from one of his sisters, George bought law books and some office furniture.

Within a few months, the two young lawyers knew their business was doomed. Beatrice was a well-established community. George and his partner were strangers in town. Beatrice citizens wanted to take their legal matters to lawyers they knew. In less than a year, George was once again unemployed.

Shortly afterwards, in September 1885, George met a man who invited him to visit Beaver City, Nebraska. A fairly new community, Beaver City didn't even have railroad facilities. George and the man had to ride through cornfields in order to get to the town. The corn "was the finest I had ever seen," George wrote later. "I had been raised on a farm, and here I was in a field that grew so tall I could not see for any distance."

The next morning, George walked up a hill overlooking the town and the surrounding farm-land. He stretched out in the short grass – called buffalo grass – and looked at the brilliant blue sky. For a long time he lay there and thought about his life.

Where was he going with his life? He was now in a place that seemed to possess everything neces-sary for the happiness and prosperity of a farmer. George had studied to be a lawyer, but he knew almost nothing about the practice of law. George knew farming. He knew land and how to make the most of it.

There are moments in life when regrets seem to lift like great iron weights, and the future is sud-denly promising – moments of renewed hope. That's what happened to George on the hill that morning in Beaver City. Maybe it was the bright blue sky.

Maybe it was the familiar, sweet smell of the earth. Maybe his heart and mind had simply endured too many disappointments.

But the life of George William Norris – the life of one of America's most influential and beloved statesmen of the 20th century – began anew when he stepped off the hill that September morning.

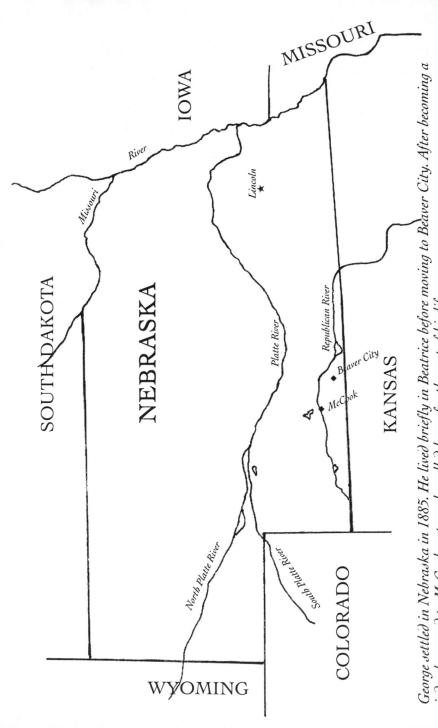

George settled in Nebraska in 1885. He lived briefly in Beatrice before moving to Beaver City. After becoming a judge he moved to McCook, a town he called home for the rest of his life.

7

A Fresh Start

George used the leftover money from his failed business in Beatrice and invested in a quarter section (160 acres) a half-mile north of Beaver City. He also opened a law office on the town square. His idea was to make a business out of the two: land and law.

Within a few months he made improvements on the land and sold it. Later in his life, he liked to say, "The first money I made in Nebraska was in the land business." The sale earned him a few hundred dollars profit. With it, he was able to start paying back his sister's loan.

Most people in Furnas County were farmers. Consequently, even non-farmers were involved in agriculture. Merchants sold farm equipment. Bankers made farm loans. Railroad workers and wagon freighters shipped crops. Everyone's fortunes, including George's, rose or fell with the farmers.

George soon made friends throughout Furnas and surrounding counties. Many of those friends — for example, David Lashley, the miller, and Dr. C.C. Greene, the town's physician and surgeon — played important roles in George's later life. Gradually his law practice took up all his time. His fees

This photograph shows three of George's Beaver City friends. George is sitting on the right.

were small, but after so many false starts, George worked as hard as if millions were involved. He was able to pay back his mother and his sister. He was also able to plan for a family.

In 1890 George married Pluma Lashley, the daughter of David and Sarah Lashley. They had courted for several months. The tall, dark-eyed Pluma was as independent-minded as her husband. For example, Pluma, who was fearless around horses, rode astride like a man, instead of side-saddle like most women.

George had never been so content with his life. He rented a four-room cottage, not far from the Lashley's big house, and he and Pluma picked out a few pieces of simple furniture. The new home was, as George later wrote, "my delight and my pride."

Ten years after he settled in Beaver City, in 1895, George's friends talked him into running for judge. Like most Ohioans at that time, George grew up supporting the Republican Party. It was the party of Abraham Lincoln. Nebraskans, who once voted for Republicans, had started to join a new political group called the Populist Party. The 1880s brought several years of drought and crop failure. Populist candidates claimed that the Republicans and big business, especially the railroads, were responsible for the farmer's troubles.

Furnas County was part of an eight-county state district. George decided to run as the Republican candidate for the judgeship in that district. His

opponent was the current judge, D. T. Welty, a
Populist.

It was a bitter contest. George campaigned all
over the eight counties. On election day, few people
believed George would win. After all, the Populists
were the majority party at that time. But when the
votes were counted – and then recounted – George
was the winner by only TWO votes.

Judge Welty protested. He demanded that
Nebraska's election commission in Lincoln, the
state capital, review the contest. Both sides gathered their evidence and headed to Lincoln. By the
time George arrived in Lincoln he discovered that
Judge Welty had dropped his allegations.

By that time, however, George had uncovered an
ugly situation that made him extremely angry:
election fraud.

8

Right and Wrong and Politics

During the campaign for judge, George visited Curtis, a town in Frontier County. There he was invited to meet with a man named A. R. Curzon, a banker and prominent Republican. Curzon led George to his private office and closed the door.

Within a year or two after the election, voters of Frontier County would once again return to the polls. This time they would decide which town – Stockville or Curtis – would be the county seat. Curzon, of course, wanted the honor for Curtis.

The banker explained all this to George and then said, "I won't support any man for judge until I know how he stands on that subject."

George could not believe what he was hearing. "His statement," George later wrote, "almost took my breath away." Curzon was "trying to induce me to make a disgraceful, dishonorable, and illegal pledge."

Curzon said that he would like to support George because he didn't think Welty had been a very good judge. Curzon added, "But I must have a promise about the county seat issue."

George told the banker that "under no circumstances would I make him or anyone else any promise as to my attitude upon any official matter that would come before me as a judge if I were so fortunate as to be elected."

As a result, Curzon became one of George's sharpest foes during the election. Curzon paid for illegal votes to be cast – called ballot-box stuffing. He handed out free whiskey to voters. George presented the evidence of this election fraud to the commission just before Welty dropped his allegations.

A year later George ran into Curzon at a Republican meeting in Omaha. The former foe was very friendly and asked to see Judge Norris in private. Curzon said he was happy that George won the election. He said he was sorry he'd fought against him and would, in the future, do everything he could to see that George was reelected.

Curzon then asked that George publicly announce that he'd erred in his earlier election-fraud charges. Curzon was once again asking George to act dishonorably. He was asking him to lie. Again the two men quarreled. George said he would not,

under any circumstances recant the charges, and that he had presented the charges to the election commission only after thorough investigation. When George refused, Curzon threatened to sue him.

"Tomorrow morning, you'll be served a summons to court," he said to George.

As Curzon stormed away, George said he'd be delighted to give the court every scrap of fraud evidence.

Curzon did not file charges. No summons was issued. A short time later Curzon moved to Boise, Idaho.

9

Change of Attitude

George and Pluma moved to McCook, Nebraska, after George won the election for judge. Forty miles west of Beaver City, their new home had its own train depot and a population of 2445 people in 1900, the biggest and most prosperous city in George's judicial district.

By the time Pluma and George moved, they had two daughters, Hazel and Marian, and were expecting a third child.

Childbirth at the end of the 19th century was often dangerous. Many women, as well as their babies, did not survive. George and Pluma counted themselves fortunate that they had two healthy girls. They were grateful, too, when a third daughter, Gertrude, was born. Unfortunately, the birth was difficult and on March 21, 1901, within a week of Gertrude's arrival, Pluma died.

His wife's death pressed on George like a crushing weight. He lost his will to live. He became so sick with grief that he stayed in bed, rarely getting up to eat or go to work. His friends were alarmed. Dr. C.C. Greene, his friend from Beaver City, came to his house and tried to help.

The doctor pleaded with his patient. "Without your assistance, I've no hope for your recovery, and I think it's up to you to decide now whether you're going to die or live."

But George refused to help himself. He later wrote, "The truth is that I had made up my mind that I did not want to live."

And then one day, as he lay in his bed, his eyes covered with a heavy cloth, he heard children playing in the side yard. He recognized Marian's voice talking with neighborhood friends. From their words he believed they were building forts with the piles of autumn leaves.

Seven-year-old Hazel, George's oldest daughter, refused to go outside with the others. She stayed in the sickroom with her father.

"Why don't you go out and play?" George asked. Though his eyes were covered, he knew she was sitting by his bed – she was always there.

Hazel said quietly that she would rather remain with her father. George tried to talk her out of staying in the dark room. He pointed out that the neighbor children had come expressly to play with her and Marian.

Finally Hazel said, "If you want me to go and play, I will, but I would rather stay here with you."

Almost half a century later, George remembered his reaction.

"Through the darkness I saw light that I had not seen before," he wrote in his autobiography. "If my little girl, then motherless, could give up the delight of playing because she wanted to sit in the darkened room with me, what must be my manhood to turn her away from my bedside?

"The thought came to me, if I died she would have no protection. What manner of man must I be to think of leaving her? So I reached over in the darkness, and took her little hand, and said:

"'Hazel, I wish you would stay here with me. If you want to stay, I would be more than pleased to have you stay.'

"I solemnly breathed a prayer then and there to live, and I think that change of attitude saved my life."

❈ *10* ❈

Campaigning and Cornhusking

One day two men from the state capital in Lincoln visited George. They were leaders in the state's Republican Party, and they wanted to talk about politics. National politics. Would Judge Norris be interested in running for his district's seat in the U.S. House of Representatives?

"You'll be running against A. C. Shallenberger," one of the men said.

George knew perfectly well the name of the opposition. A.C. Shallenberger, the district's current Representative, owned a farm but made most of his living running a bank in Alma. Both the Democrat and Populist parties supported him.

The two visitors were full of flattery – praising George's reputation as a fair and honest judge.

More than a million people had come west to stake a claim under the 1862 Homestead Act. Most of them didn't have cash to buy farm equipment and seed. And so they borrowed money from the bank, using the land as security for the loan. In recent years, hot winds, blistering heat and rainless days plagued the Great Plains. Crops failed. Farmers had trouble paying their loans. When banks weren't paid, they went to court to try to take possession of the secured land. This was called a foreclosure.

Hundreds of foreclosure cases came before Judge Norris. The law couldn't do anything about the weather, but George decided he had to take the terrible weather conditions into account. Justice had to be just. If under ordinary circumstances – good weather and a normal harvest – the farmer could pay his loan, George ordered a delay of the foreclosure. He gave the farmer a second chance to pay.

George knew why the Republicans wanted him to run. With his victory over Welty, George showed he could win against the Populists. And there was a second reason, even more important than the first.

George had been a Republican all his life. He was a passionate Republican. He always voted for Republicans – ONLY Republicans. As far as George was concerned, Democrats were nothing but troublemakers. As he later wrote, "I believed that all the virtues of government were wrapped up in the party of which I was a member, and that the only chance for pure and enlightened government was through the election of only Republicans in office."

And so George accepted the chance to unseat A.C. Shallenberger, a Democrat.

When a crowd of voters gathered to hear the two candidates debate, Shallenberger always introduced himself as a fellow farmer. Most people in the district lived on farms and earned their living from the land. Who could represent Nebraska better than a man of the soil? Shallenberger, who was also a bitter partisan, would then turn to George.

"George Norris is a lawyer," he would say. "What on earth does he know about the problems of farmers?"

George countered by saying he'd been a farmer all his life. He talked about his work as a judge – about his rulings that helped struggling farmers. He pointed out that Shallenberger was a wolf in sheep's clothing – a banker pretending to be a farmer!

And then one day, when the debate became particularly heated, he challenged Shallenberger to a contest. George stood on the bed of a wagon in front of the crowd of voters.

He had regained his strength after his illness. One of the people who helped nurse him was a young woman named Ellie Leonard. A former schoolteacher, she soon became a favorite visitor of the Norris daughters and in time she also won their father's heart. The two were married during the campaign for Fifth District's representative to Congress.

Maybe it was his renewed health and family life that gave George the nerve to say what he did as he faced the crowd.

"Gentlemen, my opponent pretends he understands the problems of common people," George said. "We both claim to be farmers. Well, let's see who's the real farmer." George turned dramatically to Shallenberger standing beside him on the wagon bed. "I challenge you, A.C. Shallenbarger, to a corn husking contest! Then we'll all see who really deserves the vote of these good farmers."

Fields of tall corn stood on either side of the road. George proposed that the two men compete

from sunrise to sunset the next day. George pledged that if he lost the husking contest he would withdraw as a candidate – with the understanding that Shallenberger would do the same if George won.

At first Shallenberger was speechless, but then he laughed as though he believed George was joking. But George continued the challenge at every debate during the rest of the campaign.

There never was a husking contest, but the idea must have appealed to many voters. George won – but barely. He received 14,927 to Shallenberger's 14,746.

Looking back on his first national campaign, George regretted that he'd exaggerated Shallenberger's weaknesses as a representative of the Fifth District. George was also ashamed of his cornhusking challenge. He later wrote that it was "unstatesmanlike [and] foolish."

Ellie Leonard (above), George's second wife, was a young school-teacher in McCook. George had known her for several years due to his interest in schools. When George was well enough to travel after his illness, he went to California to meet Ellie's parents. On July 8, 1903, in San Jose, California, they were married. Their honeymoon was in Wisconsin. While there, George bought an island in Rainbow Lake where he later built a cabin, which would host the L. U. N. reunions each summer until 1943. (See page 18)

※ *11* ※

A New Man in Congress

Washington, D. C. was a swamp in 1903.
The stately Capitol building was built of
white marble in 1829, but the streets were still
unpaved and often muddy. George Norris rented a
room at the YMCA (Young Men's Christian Asso-
ciation). Ellie and the girls stayed behind in
McCook. His two-year term as a member of the
U.S. House of Representatives didn't pay enough to
maintain two residences.

One of the important jobs of the House of Representatives is to pass bills – potential laws. A bill is
created in one of the many House committees, made
up of the elected representatives, before it is presented for vote to the entire House. A bill becomes
a law when – and if – both houses of Congress (the
House and Senate) pass the bill and the President
signs it.

George wanted to serve on the Public Grounds and Buildings (PGB) Committee, a group that initiated projects in the nation's capital.

At that time most of the members of the House were Republicans. As the majority party, they had the right to choose the Speaker of the House, who acted as the representatives' leader. One of the first meetings George attended in Washington D.C. was the Republican Party Caucus. Each party had its own caucus, and George learned that party members were expected to follow strictly the decisions of their caucus. In 1903 the Republican Caucus voted for Joseph Cannon, a Republican from Illinois, as Speaker of the House. George gladly supported the choice. The Speaker's job was very influential. Speaker Cannon was responsible for appointing – and refusing to reappoint – members of the committees. George was happy when Speaker Cannon selected him for the PGB Committee.

When George's committee met for the first time, the members talked about putting together a large building bill. Everyone realized that the nation's capital needed sprucing up. One committee member asked if they should begin drafting the bill.

George thought the question was odd. Of course they should draft legislation. That was their job. George was surprised when the chairman of the committee and other members, including Democrats, said they'd need to wait for Speaker Cannon's permission to write the bill.

What did Cannon have to do with writing bills for the PGB Committee? George wondered. Cannon worked on another committee. He had made himself chairman of the Rules Committee. It was the most powerful committee in the House. The Rules Committee wrote the House agenda, the calendar that showed when bills would be discussed and voted upon. If the Rules Committee refused to put a bill on the agenda then that bill could never go through the House – could never, therefore, become a law.

When Speaker Cannon sent his approval, George and his fellow committee members began work on the building bill. George spent weeks researching and writing parts of the bill. He did not have the chance to see the entire bill before it was presented to the House.

The final bill shocked George. Dozens of additions had been written into it. The additions had nothing to do with public grounds and buildings. Cannon and others had inserted a long list of special projects – including a railroad subsidy, a munitions contract and a turkey farm! These projects were favors to people who had helped Cannon and his friends get elected. Such additions to bills are called "pork barrel."

George wasn't naïve. He knew that people who helped political candidates get elected often expected special consideration. George remembered his campaign for judge when A. R. Curzon tried to influence him. But he didn't realize that some of the nation's most powerful and respected lawmakers would turn the nation's laws into instruments of political favors.

George had much to learn.

Later, when a bill to observe George Washington's birthday was introduced to the House, he supported it. He thought his vote was patriotic. But the members of the Republican Caucus were outraged. Democrats had sponsored the bill. George was the only Republican to vote for it. After all, he thought, a stately portrait of General Washington was hanging in the House chamber. Didn't it make sense to honor the first president with a birthday observance?

George listened to his conscience. He complained about pork barrel. He voted for a Democrat bill. He acted independently of his party's leaders.

Most members of his caucus stopped talking to him. Someone sent him a message advising him against being disloyal to the party. George understood the threat. He was just a junior Representative from Nebraska. If he didn't start going along with the party caucus, the powerful Speaker Cannon would make sure that he wasn't reelected. And George understood something else.

If he wanted to return to the House of Representative *and* to vote his conscience, he would have to bring down the Speaker.

12

The Battle for Power

George looked up at the clock above the wide double doors leading into the House of Representatives. It was fifteen minutes until one o'clock. He unbuttoned his suit coat. Was it getting hot or was it just his nervousness? He put his hand inside his coat and felt for the paper tucked inside his vest pocket.

It was Thursday, March 17, 1910. What would happen within the next hour would change George's life. It would also change history.

John Dalzell of Pennsylvania sat in the Speaker's seat. Speaker Cannon was at a meeting and couldn't preside over the House this afternoon. Dalzell, one of the old-guard Republicans, was Cannon's substitute. The old guard didn't like George's independent attitude. Dalzell said he was hotheaded and, like Cannon, never called on him when the Nebraskan wanted to speak or make a

motion. He ignored him. He allowed other, less independent congressmen have the floor.

For a while George thought he alone resented the power of Speaker Cannon. But a few weeks earlier Rep. Augustus Gardner, Republican from Massachusetts, stopped George in the cloakroom. He congratulated the Nebraskan on standing up to Cannon and told George that several other young Republicans agreed with him. They, too, resented the autocratic Cannon.

Newspapers took notice of the rebels among the Republicans. The press called them "insurgents." In time, George and the others became known as the Progressives.

Cannon had a very effective weapon against his enemies: the rules of the House. The rules helped keep the daily business of the House organized. For example, limits were placed on debates and on the number of changes, or amendments, to a bill. A bill had to be on the calendar before it could be debated. Bills were also scheduled in a certain order – the agenda – and could not be debated out of order.

Some insurgents hated the rules, but George appreciated the need for rules. He'd learned to play – and win! – by the rules as a young debater in Ohio. And besides, George had a plan to use the rules as his own weapon.

Dalzell pulled out his pocket watch and checked the time. He looked across the chamber at the clock above the doors. George followed Dalzell's gaze. The Pennsylvania representative was a precise man. He never wavered from his lunch schedule. At exactly one o'clock, Dalzell would walk out of the chamber and go downstairs to the coffeshop where he would have a sandwich, coffee and pie. During Dalzell's lunch break, Representative Walter Smith would preside over the House. Although he wasn't an insurgent, Smith had always treated George respectfully.

At that moment a man named Edgar Crumpacker from Indiana was speaking. Crumpacker, chairman of the Committee on Census, was presenting a bill that called for taking the new census. (The U.S. Constitution directs that all the people in the country be counted every ten years. From this record, the federal government

makes sure all Americans are being represented.)
Through an oversight, Crumpacker's bill was over-
looked during an earlier session of the House. The
House needed to take action on the bill immediately
so that the census could begin. Though the bill was
far down the House's agenda, Cannon had allowed
it to be presented out of order. Several people had
objected to Cannon's decision, but, as usual, the
Speaker overruled the objections.

George didn't hear a word Crumpacker said. He
was more interested in Dalzell. The Pennsylvania
congressman looked again at his watch and then at
the big wall clock. It was five seconds until one
o'clock. Dalzell rose from his chair, handed Smith
the gavel and headed for the chamber exit. Smith
sat down and took up the presiding post.

George stopped breathing. He clutched the
edge of his desk, afraid that his hands might start to
shake. When Dalzell reached the exit, George
walked toward Smith and quietly asked for permission to speak. Crumpacker was still talking, but his
allotted time was almost up. Smith said George
could have the floor for five minutes after
Crumpacker finished.

George barely made it back to his chair when
Smith called on him. Taking the paper from his
pocket, George read a resolution. It called for the
complete overhaul of the Rules Committee rules.
The last sentence of the resolution was "That the

Speaker should not be a member of the Committee on Rules."

George later described the moment: "I remember a feeling of curious detachment from the ripple of surprise, and the new tenseness that set in, as the resolution was read. I had formulated no definite battle lines although I had weighed the possibilities with great care. So in that moment it seemed to me triumph was near...I had waited so long, watchful day after day during weeks of weary frustration, for the opportunity I felt would present itself in good season. Here it was. Every member of the House knew full well the stakes of this battle."

Someone shouted, "Against the rules!" Others joined in yelling that George didn't have the right to speak. His resolution wasn't on the agenda. He and his resolution were out of order.

None of George's insurgent friends knew about his plans. But as the explosion of his resolution spread throughout the house, he could see their faces light up. They understood his strategy.

Gardner shouted above the noise, "The Speaker allowed the census bill out of order. What's good for the goose is good for the gander!"

Under the House rules, the Speaker could decide that George's resolution was out of order, which is what Cannon did. After all, George's resolution would strip Speaker Cannon of much of his power. According to the House rules, George had a right to appeal the Speaker's decision and then the issue would come before the House for a vote.

And that is what happened. All the Republican insurgents and Democrats voted for George's resolution. It passed, 191 to 156.

When Cannon saw the results of the vote, he submitted his resignation as Speaker but the House voted against it. George surprised his friends when he refused to vote with them.

"I had no personal feeling against the Speaker," George later said. "My opposition was solely to his frightful abuse of power...I had not prepared that resolution to punish an individual. I was shooting at the system. I wanted simply to take from Mr. Cannon the autocratic powers which his office...had conferred upon him."

The downfall of the Speaker made national news. Within a few days, George Norris's picture was in newspapers across the country. Everyone knew the name of the junior Representative from Nebraska who brought down the mighty Joseph Cannon.

13

"Just a little something for yourself"

One day in 1911 a lobbyist visited George in Washington D.C. The lobbyist worked for several railroad companies and liquor companies. It was no secret that he and the companies he represented fought against the insurgents and gave campaign money to politicians, both Republicans and Democrats, who worked to pass laws that helped big companies.

George Norris's fifth term in the House of Representatives was coming to an end in 1912. He decided not to run again. Some of his friends wanted him to run for governor of Nebraska. Some wanted him to run for the U.S. Senate.

George dreaded another election of any kind. His leadership role among the insurgents made him extremely unpopular with many influential Republicans in Nebraska. To make matters worse, George

was campaigning *against* the Republicans' presidential candidate, Pres. William Howard Taft.

George supported Theodore Roosevelt, who was not only a former Republican but was also a former U.S. president. Favoring social and economic reform, Roosevelt had established the Progressive Party. He favored policies such as regulating big business, ending child labor, the eight-hour work day, women's suffrage and the conservation of the country's natural resources – forests, soil, water power, coal and other minerals. George believed in many of these policies.

And so George wondered why the lobbyist would visit him – the best-known progressive in the House. In the last election, the lobbyist backed the Democrat candidate for Nebraska governor. George was, therefore, surprised when the man said he wanted to talk to George about running for governor.

The lobbyist painted a bright picture. George didn't have to do anything but announce his candidacy for governor. The companies would handle everything. They'd provide all the campaign money. The lobbyist nodded to a small suitcase by his chair. He said it contained $15,000, and he would give it to George if he agreed to the deal.

"This isn't campaign money," the man said. "Just a little something for yourself and that nice family of yours."

George's face darkened. He said the man had the wrong politician. He said he supported government regulation of big business.

"We're aren't requiring any promises," the man said.

How strange, George thought. If the companies the man represented didn't care whether or not he supported their interests, why on earth would they want to get him elected as Nebraska's governor?

And then the answer dawned on him. The lobbyist and his companies were afraid George was planning to run for the U.S. Senate – and that he would win! George later wrote, "They would rather have me in the governorship than in the United States Senate, where they thought I would be more injurious to their ideas of government."

George told the man to take his suitcase and leave. George had no interest in his bribe or his offer to run for Nebraska governor.

The next day George announced his candidacy for U.S. Senator.

❦ *14* ❦

United States Senator

At the time George ran for the office, U.S. Senators were elected by state legislatures, although the senatorial candidates' names appeared on the ballot. Amendment 17 of the Constitution, providing for the popular election of Senators, didn't become law until 1913. Consequently, when senatorial candidates ran for office they didn't try to campaign to the general voters, but rather to the few state legislators who controlled the election outcome.

Many Nebraskans wanted to change the Constitution, and so the state had adopted what was called the "Oregon Plan." Under this arrangement, candidates for the state legislature had the option of having a statement printed next to their names on the official ballot. The statement said that, if elected, they would vote for the senatorial candidate who received the most popular votes. Nearly every Nebraska legislative candidate chose this plan.

Although many people in his party fought against him, George won the Republican Senate nomination. The Democrats ran one of George's former political opponents: A.C. Shallenberger. The two men fought hard. They wanted the popular vote because they trusted that the winning legislative candidates would honor their pledge.

When the votes were counted, George won the popular vote by 38,071. But the Democrats won the majority of seats in the Nebraska legislature that year. Many Democrat leaders tried to persuade their newly elected members to break their "Oregon Plan" pledge and pick Shallenberger, although he had lost the popular vote. But the effort failed.

Nebraskans sent George to the Senate.

George's political friend, however, lost. That year the Republican Party was deeply divided, some voted for Taft, some for Roosevelt. The new president was the Democrat, Woodrow Wilson, who won by only 42% of the popular vote.

❄ 15 ❄

Sowing Seeds
for a Future Harvest

When George was sworn into office in March, 1913, he was one of the nation's leading progressives. At that time, progressives wanted to reform government in three main ways: rid the government of corruption; expand democratic rights to more Americans; and improve the lives of poor people.

George was enthusiastic. For one thing, Ellie and the girls had moved to Washington D.C. During the last ten years, George had stayed at the YMCA, but now as a Senator with a six-year term of office, he could afford to have his family with him.

He was also enthusiastic because the newly elected Congress favored many of his progressive ideas. Pres. Wilson even initiated a reform program called "New Freedom."

In the Senate, George was appointed to the Public Lands Committee. In this committee, George worked on a very difficult problem. Every year in the spring, many United States rivers, especially the Mississippi and Tennessee Rivers, flooded their banks. The rising waters destroyed homes and businesses and washed away rich topsoil. Whole towns washed away. People lost their lives. After a flood, the US government had to pay billions of dollars repairing the damage and helping people.

Soon after George joined the Public Lands Committee the Senate debated a bill that provided $10 million for the upgrading of the lower Mississippi River channel. The money would pay for dikes, levees and dredged channels. Supporters of the bill insisted that by spending a large sum of money at

one time, many states along the southern end of the river would be spared yearly floods.

In the past, Congress funded programs that deepened and straightened river channels and built dikes. But these measures had little effect. George believed this new bill was just a larger version of those earlier efforts.

George wanted to do something unusual. He believed the entire river valley needed to be altered in order to prevent flooding. Dams should be built in the nation's mountain ranges where major rivers received their water from melting snow or big storms. When people needed water, the dams could release it slowly.

Three years before George went to the Senate the Pathfinder Dam in Wyoming was opened. It held back floodwaters on the North Platte River. Farmers along the river valley watered their crops with the dam's released water. Taxpayers paid for the dam. According to federal law, farmers who used the spill-off had to pay back the entire cost of its construction.

George realized that the Pathfinder Dam not only provided irrigation water, but also held back some of the water that would eventually find its way to the lower Mississippi River. The Wyoming dam was helping people in the south. In other words, the Pathfinder was helping solve the problems that the new bill in the Senate was trying to solve.

So why should the farmers alone have to pay for the dam? Why not use some of the $10 million to pay for Pathfinder Dam?

George proposed an amendment to the new bill. It stated that the federal government would pay for half the cost of Pathfinder. The farmers would pay the rest.

George didn't expect the amendment to pass. Many engineers said George's idea wouldn't work. Many lawmakers said it was too expensive. And so George was surprised and pleased when his amendment failed to pass by a small margin.

But it wasn't over. This early defeat was the opening chapter to one of George's greatest victories. In time he would live to see his dam-building idea embraced by America's finest engineers. He would live to see his idea become a scientifically accepted approach to flood control. He would live to see it increase farm production. His idea would lessen the destruction of floods, expand irrigation, free up semi-arid regions for farm families, and increase food production for the nation and the world.

But all that was in the future.

Right now the battles on the floor of the Senate suddenly seemed insignificant. Far away across the Atlantic Ocean a much bigger battle erupted – and it was about to engulf America.

❧ 16 ❧

The Great War

On June 28, 1914, Archduke Francis Ferdinand of Austria and his wife, Sophie, arrived in Sarajevo, the capital of Bosnia. The Austrian-Hungarian government recently had added Bosnia to its Empire. One of Bosnia's nationalists, who hated the take-over of his country, leaped into the royal motorcade and shot to death the archduke and duchess.

When the news of the deaths reached Washington, D.C., few people thought the incident would lead to World War I. But tensions, based primarily on power struggles, had been growing for many years in Europe. By the end of summer, several countries declared war on their neighbors. In the end, the Allied Powers (Great Britain, France, Russia and others) were at war with the Central Powers (Germany, Austria-Hungary, Bulgaria and the Ottoman Empire).

Leaders in the U.S. tried to keep America out of the conflict. Why should the U.S. get involved in a matter so remote? Pres. Wilson promised neutrality.

But neutrality was difficult. The U.S. had political and trade agreements with many of the countries, especially with Great Britain. And then German submarines – U-boats – began firing on U.S. civilian ships. On May 7, 1915, a U-boat sank the British passenger liner, the Lusitania, the largest and fastest ship in the world, sailing off the coast of southern Ireland. Of the 1,924 passengers and crew, 1,198 died – 144 were Americans.

Despite his promise for neutrality, Pres. Wilson asked Congress to arm U.S. trading ships. He believed the endangered ships needed some means of protection. By that time, most members of Congress favored taking action against the Central Powers.

George was not one of those people. He was an isolationist, a person who believes in staying out of foreign affairs. George bitterly opposed any U.S. military involvement. Turning merchant ships into battle-ready ships was inviting disaster. George also believed that only large companies selling military supplies would be the winners of an American involvement. Why should young Americans die so that large companies could get rich? he asked.

George and 11 other isolationist Senators knew that Pres. Wilson's request had enough votes in Congress to pass. The isolationists had to find some way to keep Congress from voting.

❧ *17* ❧

Filibuster

Many Senators recently had won election based on their support of Pres. Wilson's neutrality promise. George and his minority of 11 hoped the new Senators would join the Norris opposition. Unfortunately those Senators hadn't been sworn into office yet. Pres. Wilson had asked for support from the lame duck Congress, made up of many people who hadn't won reelection.

In those days, Congress and the President officially came into office in March, four months after their election in November of the previous year. Consequently, during that four months, officeholders who haven't been reelected – lame ducks – could still make policy and pass laws.

George and his friends were determined to keep the current Senate from voting on Pres. Wilson's request. And so they decided to take a drastic parliamentary step. They filibustered.

69

Filibuster is a strategy to delay a vote by giving a very long speech. When Senators filibuster, they deliberately keep control of the Senate so that nothing else can happen. Filibustering is a way that Senators with unpopular views can get their points across. But filibustering is also unpopular because it allows a rebellious minority to halt the work of the entire Senate.

Two important circumstances made the success of a filibuster possible. First, any Senator could debate an issue for as long as he wanted. Unlike the House, the Senate didn't put time limitations on its members — at least not in 1917. Second, a bill automatically dies if it is not voted upon before the session of a lame duck Senate ends. In that year the session ended at noon on March 4.

The bill was brought before the Senate on March 1, 1917.

George was chosen floor leader of the bill's opposition. Another Nebraskan, Sen. Gilbert M. Hitchcock, was floor leader of the supporters. Unknown to the rest of the Senate, George and his 11 friends had prepared for battle.

When George began his side of the debate, he alone, the Senate rules said, had the right to call on others to speak. George planned to call on only the isolationists. And he carefully had scheduled the timing of those 11 speakers so there would be no break in the discussion. A break would end the filibuster and allow for a motion to vote. George

and his friends had to hold the floor for 72 hours – non-stop, day and night.

When the bill's supporters realized what George and his friends intended to do, they were angry. Senators shouted abuse at the filibusters. Some warned George that the people of Nebraska would never vote for him again. The threat was real because most Americans now favored entering the war and fighting the Germans.

The supporters of the bill made their own plan. One of them would remain in the Senate chamber at all times. They wanted to seize upon the slightest halt in the filibuster.

George and the opposition went on talking – and talking.

George later wrote, "During the night, I remained at the Senate chamber to guard against eventualities. The hours of darkness dragged slowly. To fill out the time, I consumed two or three hours of discussion myself. I was talking when the first tints of the sunrise colored the eastern sky and the mists which overhung the Potomac."

By late afternoon on the third day, George and his friends realized that the filibuster would succeed. Their joy only further enraged the bill's supporters.

"Those final minutes live in my memory," George wrote. "In that chamber, men became slaves to emotion. The clash of anger and bitterness, in my judgement, never has been exceeded in the history of the United States Senate...The hour hand dragged toward twelve, and when it pointed to the arrival of noon, the chair announced adjournment. The filibuster had won."

The anger of his colleagues depressed George because he felt they were not giving him "credit for being either honest or patriotic." For the rest of his life, George believed he was right to filibuster. But many others condemned the act. Every newspaper in Nebraska denounced him. His fellow Nebraskans even doubted his sanity. Some called him a traitor.

And then George did something very dramatic – and very brave.

※ *18* ※

"I have come home to tell you the truth"

George rented an auditorium in Lincoln, Nebraska, and called a public meeting. He invited everyone. He said he wanted to explain why he had filibustered and defeated Pres. Wilson's plan to arm merchant ships. He said that if the voters still felt he was wrong after they heard his explanation then he would resign as their Senator. He said he was unwilling to "represent the people of Nebraska if they did not want me."

Republicans from Omaha and Lincoln urged him to stay in Washington D.C. They warned him not to come to Nebraska. They predicted a riot if he showed his face. Others said George was so unpopular that no one would come to the meeting.

None of George's friends would accompany him when he walked to the auditorium on that spring night in 1917.

"I cannot remember a day in my life," he later wrote, "when I have suffered more from a lonely feeling of despondency."

The auditorium was packed. Though against the fire code, the police allowed the overflow to sit in the aisles. George expected an unfriendly audience. What he got was utter silence. Not a single hiss. Not a single handclap.

George stood at the podium. For a moment he said nothing. He looked out at the silent faces of his fellow Nebraskans. He was nervous, but his voice was soft and calm when he finally spoke.

"I have come home to tell you the truth," he began simply.

The response was amazing. George described it in his autobiography: "Immediately there was a burst of applause from all parts of the audience. Never in my lifetime has applause done me the good that did."

George went on to tell why he had opposed the U.S. entering the war. For years he had carried with him the last letter written by his older brother, John Henry, the one killed in the Civil War. He remembered the grief the young man's death had caused his family. George could understand why his brother and others had taken up arms in that long ago war. Union soldiers, like his brother, fought and died to keep the country together. But he could not understand why U.S. soldiers should have to die in a European war.

A half century after George gave his speech, a young man named John F. Kennedy, who would one day become a U.S. President, wrote a book called *Profiles in Courage*. In the book he said, "George Norris hated war – and he feared that `Big Business'… was bent on driving the nation into a useless, bloody struggle…and he was resentful of the manner in which [Wilson's bill] was being steamrollered through the Congress. It is not now important whether Norris was right or wrong. What is now important is the courage he displayed in support of his convictions."

There was no special election. There was no resignation. Although many Nebraskans disagreed with him, they trusted and admired George for standing up for his beliefs. And they would go on trusting and admiring – and reelecting – him for the next 32 years.

Prosperity and Poverty

The 1920s, often called the Jazz Age, was a time of prosperity for many Americans. The administrations of Warren Harding and Calvin Coolidge, presidents during the 1920s, wanted to do everything possible to help businesses. They convinced Congress to lower taxes on the wealthy. Many people in government believed that if the rich paid lower taxes, they would use their money to build more factories. This, in turn, would provide jobs and income for poor people.

Pres. Coolidge said, "The business of the United States is business." During his years in office, the country prospered. Factory production, especially in automobile plants, increased more than 30 percent. Henry Ford, who developed the assembly line for producing cars, became a national hero. Wages for many Americans rose. The rising stock market provided opportunities for Americans with money to invest. Faith in big business grew stronger than ever before.

George was glad for the prosperity. But something began to bother him. Because he often traveled between Washington, D.C. and McCook, Nebraska, George saw that many people living in rural areas hadn't benefited from the prosperity. Unlike people in big cities, they didn't have factory jobs. Without good wages they couldn't afford to buy stocks or cars or even electricity for their homes. Farm families, 25% of the population, lived in poverty. Crop prices were low. Coal miners, too, suffered. Oil was replacing coal as a fuel source. Textile workers lost jobs when fashion changed from long skirts to short in the Jazz Age.

In 1926 George was in Pennsylvania campaigning for a candidate for the U.S. Senate. During that campaign an incident occurred that he remembered for the rest of his life.

One day a man and boy showed up to drive George to his next speaking engagement. The man's face was black, except for a small white spot on his left cheek. His spine was twisted like a fishing hook. He had worked in coal mines all of his life.

"Years before," George wrote later, "in an explosion that killed many miners, he was so terribly injured...Both arms, both legs, and his collarbone had been broken – one arm in two places. The force of the mine blast had injured his spinal cord, jammed his head out of shape, and seared every exposed spot on his body black."

Now unable to work, the miner devoted his life to helping miners.

While the miner told George his story, they passed a cemetery. The man pointed to a small tombstone in the back corner. It was the grave of a Civil War veteran who worked as a coal miner after the war.

George's driver wanted the senator to visit the grave. He particularly wanted George to read the epitaph cut in the stone. The old miner buried there had worked hard all of his life but had died a pauper.

The black-faced miner said that hard work did not save any miner from poverty. At that time, coal workers had to live in houses owned by the coal companies. They had to buy food and other supplies at stores owned by the companies. The cost of rent and food was always higher than the miners' paychecks. Thus, the workers were continually in debt to their bosses.

Coal companies also required that miners keep a small amount of money on deposit in case they were injured or died before the debt was paid. When the man, who had three children, was hurt in the explosion, his wife tried to collect the deposit to help with expenses, but the company refused. Without the assistance of neighbors, the family would have starved.

❦ 20 ❦

Muscle Shoals

George sat at his desk reading S.J. Res. 49. He knew every word in the resolution. He had written it. In part the resolution aimed "to provide for the national defense by the creation of a corporation for the operation of the government properties at or near Muscle Shoals and for other purposes."

It was a plan to build a major dam, an old dream of George's. This was his third attempt to get the bill into law. His first resolution in 1926 never made it to Congress for a vote. His second resolution became a bill in 1927, but it was vetoed by Pres. Coolidge. George hoped a third attempt in 1929 would succeed now that a new president, Herbert Hoover, was in office.

Muscle Shoals was on the Tennessee River as it flowed through northwestern Alabama. During World War I, the government spent $150,000,000 to build a plant there, which included Wilson Dam. At the plant the government hoped to produce nitrate, used in making explosives for bombs. But before the dam was finished, the war ended. Congress lost interest in the project.

Henry Ford offered to buy Muscle Shoals for $5,000,000. George was one of the few people who didn't want the Ford Motor Company to own the

plant. Instead of selling it to Ford, George had a better idea. He wanted the government to complete Wilson Dam. George remembered the congressional battles over Pathfinder Dam. He never gave up his idea that damming many of the nation's waterways would help solve flood problems. Controlling the release of water would also provide electricity to rural America. Most people living in the Alabama and Tennessee countryside didn't have electricity. Why not use the dam to generate cheap electricity for people in the south?

Even after Henry Ford withdrew his offer to buy Muscle Shoals, members of Congress still opposed George's idea. They didn't want the government involved in dam building. They supported the power companies which feared that government-owned dams would cut into their profits. George pointed out that most people living in the Tennessee Valley region were too poor to buy the companies' electricity.

George's third bill passed the House and the Senate. But within a short time the bill died when Pres. Hoover vetoed it.

And that might have been the end of it – except for a terrible thing that happened just five months after George proposed S.J. Res. 49.

The shaded area marks the boundary of the region served by the TVA.

The TVA was the first time a federal agency was directed to address the total resource development needs of a major region. The TVA took in the whole Tennessee River basin, about 41,000 square miles covering parts of seven states. The TVA's main offices are located in the region, rather than in Washington, D.C. This allows it to maintain a close working relationship with the people of the region.

In 1998 the TVA generated more electricity than any other U.S. utility, supplying eight million residents. There are 50 dams in the hydroelectric system with a capacity of more than six million kilowatts.

Legend:
— = Dam
* = Power Plant
Several of the TVA dams and power plants are shown on the map.

ILLINOIS, MISSOURI, ARKANSAS, KENTUCKY, VIRGINIA, NORTH CAROLINA, SOUTH CAROLINA, GEORGIA, TENNESSEE, ALABAMA, MISSISSIPPI

Norris Dam, Wilson Dam, Muscle Shoals

Atlanta, Birmingham, Nashville, Bowling Green, Huntsville, Memphis, Tupelo, Oxford

Tennessee River, Mississippi River

❧ *21* ❧

Dark Days and Dirty Tricks

When Herbert Hoover took office in March, 1929, he announced, "We in America are nearer to the final triumph over poverty than ever before in the history of the land." He believed that the long prosperity of the Jazz Age would continue. But on October, 1929, the New York Stock Market collapsed.

The Great Depression had begun.

Farmers watched the prices for their crops fall to almost nothing. Coal prices dropped, too, and miners lost their jobs. Factory workers and laborers also lost their jobs when employers couldn't pay their wages. Thousands of unemployed homeless people built shacks out of cardboard and old cars. All over the country these shantytowns were called "Hoovervilles."

"It is not a credit to human intelligence that conditions of this character can prevail in this world," George wrote. "Somehow, in some manner, there should be the intelligence, the human capacity, to avoid the tragedy of a great abundance accompanied by a great hunger.

"Poverty there is, and poverty there always will be, men say – hunger and starvation, desperation and futility. That is not a civilized state…Poverty and hunger breed desperation, and desperation breeds contempt for law, and contempt for law breeds anarchy…"

Hundreds of "Hoovervilles" sprang up around the country during the Depression. This one was in Paterson, New Jersey, on Molly Jan Brook. Its residents were out-of-work laborers from a local silk factory.

George wanted to pass laws to bring relief to the farmers and people in the Hoovervilles.

That was a lofty ideal. It would produce some of the most important legislation of the 20th century.

But in 1930 it also produced powerful enemies.

George came to Washington D.C. in 1903 as a loyal Republican. He was strongly partisan. Republicans could do no wrong, he believed. Democrats could do no right.

But George had changed. He served ten years in the House of Representatives as a Republican. He ran as a Republican for the Senate four times. Through those years, he learned that both parties were capable of good and bad. After a while he didn't prefer one party more than the other. If the Democrats supported a bill George wanted passed, then he worked with Democrats. If a Republican introduced a bill George favored, he helped to pass that bill.

He fought against Pres. Woodrow Wilson, not because Wilson was a Democrat but because Wilson wanted to involve the U.S. in World War I. George fought against the election of Herbert Hoover, a Republican, for the same reason. He disagreed strongly with Hoover's policies.

George admired Pres. Theodore Roosevelt – not because he was a Republican. Until he met Roosevelt, George had never considered the importance of the federal government taking the leading role in preserving natural resources such as water, coal and soil.

When he met the coal miner in Pennsylvania, George was campaigning for the Democrat candidate for Senator. He strongly objected to the

Republican candidate, W.H. Vare, a millionaire who controlled the state's political machine. Vare was everything that George disliked in American politics.

Republican leaders in Nebraska and elsewhere were tired of George's independence. When he ran for re-election to the Senate in 1930, Republicans decided to take action.

A group of Republican Party leaders found a young grocery store manager in Broken Bow, Nebraska, named George W. Norris. The leaders paid the grocer $500 and registered him as a candidate in the Senate race. The grocer and his backers knew that he had no hope of winning – but with his name on the ballot, neither did Sen. George W. Norris. Two George W. Norrises on the ballot would create confusion. Consequently, all of the votes for either George W. Norris would be thrown out.

When Senator Norris learned of the plot, he called it a "dastardly trick." Luckily, the trick did no real harm. "Grocer" Norris's registration to run for Senate arrived at the Nebraska election office two days after the deadline. Therefore, his name couldn't go on the ballot.

The scheme, which was eventually investigated by the U.S. Congress, failed to defeat the Senator. He easily won the election by more than 70,000 votes. Nor did the scheme dampen his independent spirit.

22

*Lame Ducks
and Yellow Dogs*

When George returned to Washington, D.C. in 1930, he continued working on bills that his conscience – not his party affiliation – believed in.

George wanted to shorten the period of time between the election and the day a newly elected person took office. The four months from November to March, called the lame duck session of Congress, posed many problems. Sometimes lame duck officials – ones who hadn't been elected but were still in office – were willing to pass laws they knew the voters opposed.

George wrote, "This gave any President ...enormous power over legislation. On several occasions, it was revealed, many of these lame-duck members of Congress were willing to follow the command of the executive [the President] and to adopt legislation which he desired. For their subservience, they

89

were given fat executive appointments."

George first began his fight to pass the lame duck bill in 1922. For more than 10 years the bill continually died in Congress. George's election victory in 1930 strengthened his determination to fight on. On December 9, 1931, he again introduced his resolution.

Congress had changed with the 1930 election. Voters around the country, shaken by the stock market crash, had sent many new officials to Washington, D.C. Both houses of Congress quickly passed the bill. Within four months, the bill – a proposed amendment to the Constitution – went to each state legislature for ratification.

On January 23, 1933 – less than 10 months later – enough states ratified and the 20th Amendment, also called the Lame Duck Law, became law. The newly elected president and members of Congress took office in January, rather than in March.

But George wasn't finished.

He remembered the black-faced miner he'd met in Pennsylvania. The hard life described by the miner resembled the lives of countless people all over the country. For many years the senator had tried to get a law passed that would help miners, but lame duck sessions of Congress had killed his efforts. George tried again in 1932.

George wanted to end "yellow dog" contracts. Mine owners required that all workers sign these contracts. Under a yellow dog contract, a miner agreed not to ask for a pay increase or for better working conditions. The miner agreed not to meet with other miners for the purpose of talking about better conditions. The yellow dog contract forbade a miner from joining a labor union or from associating with union organizers.

Mining companies formed partnerships to enforce the contracts. If a miner, unhappy with the conditions at one mine, left his job or was fired, no other mine would hire him. Even the country's justice system supported the mine companies. If a miner tried to break his contract – that is, talked about increasing his pay or joining a union – the mining company got the courts to stop him. Miners were often jailed.

By signing a yellow dog contract the miner signed away his rights as an American. George called it slavery.

During the 1920s, Congress wasn't interested in passing anti-business legislation. But now, with the Depression, the American people sympathized with the hardships of workers. Support for George's yellow dog contract bill gained support in Congress.

When the bill reached the Senate, George gave a speech. In it he quoted the epitaph from the old miner's gravestone he'd seen in Pennsylvania:

"For 40 years beneath the sod,
with pick and spade I did my task,
The coal king's slave, but now,
thank God, I'm free at last."

One Kansas woman described the dust storms: "When we opened the door, swirling whirlwinds of soil beat against us unmercifully. The dust seeped into cupboards and closets. It turned everyone's hair gray and stiff. We ground dirt between our teeth." An estimated million people fled their homes from Texas to the Dakotas during the Dust Bowl years.

While George focused on passage in the Senate, a representative named Fiorella La Guardia worked to get the bill passed in the House of Representatives. George and LaGuardia were Republicans.

That was almost all they had in common. One was a farmer from the midwest. The other was a New Yorker. And yet they formed one of the most important partnerships in Congressional history. During the 1930s, they worked together on other bills to help farmers, miners and city workers.

The yellow dog contract bill passed both houses of Congress. Pres. Hoover, who had threatened to veto the bill, signed it. In what became known as the Norris-La Guardia Act, miners – all laborers – gained their full rights as American citizens.

The yellow dog contract law helped workers, but it didn't solve the nation's economic problems. Pres. Hoover hoped to build people's confidence. But Americans were afraid. They didn't believe the President when he said, "Recovery is just around the corner." In the 1932 election they voted in a new president: Franklin Roosevelt.

Still the nation's fears grew worse. From 1934 to 1939, a terrible drought hit the Great Plains. Crops died. Without rain, the topsoil dried up and blew away. What few crops could grow were eaten by plagues of grasshoppers. Farmers couldn't earn enough money to pay their mortgages, so banks foreclosed on farms.

Roosevelt said he had a New Deal, a plan for recovery.

And then he told Americans, "The only thing we have to fear is fear itself."

After the dirty tricks of the 1930 election, people wondered if George would leave the Republican Party. This political cartoon shows George being confronted with the question of whether he will run as a third party candidate in the 1932 presidential election.

A natural choice for national leadership, George was a statesman. He spent his career working to pass laws that helped disenfranchised people who were in need, even if those people weren't from his home state of Nebraska.

No More Fear

Just one year before Roosevelt's election, George tried a fourth time to get his flood-control bill through Congress. No action was taken.

But as the Depression and Dustbowl years continued, the American people were tired of delays. George's bill offered a way to relieve droughts and control floods. Dams along rivers and streams could control floods by holding back water. At times of drought, when people needed water, the dams could release the reserved water.

Right after Pres. Roosevelt came into office, George tried a fifth time. His bill, now called the Tennessee Valley Authority (TVA), passed.

Within 11 years, nine giant dams were completed along the Tennessee River, and several more were under construction. The TVA eventually saved three million acres of land from erosion. It increased the average income of people in the re-

*George is standing in front of Norris Dam, the first con-
structed by the TVA. Its construction began only a few months after
the agency was created in 1933. Three years later, its completion
helped control the disastrous Ohio and Mississippi River flood of
1937. At 285 feet tall, the dam is one of the tallest of the TVA.*

---

gion by tenfold. Every penny that taxpayers paid to
build the dams was repaid through the sale of
power.

Three years after TVA began, the Rural Electri-
fication Administration (REA) was created. This
project brought electricity to rural America. George

introduced a bill, which Congress eventually passed, that made the REA permanent and nation-wide.

George knew first hand about the long hours and grinding work faced by farm families. His mother, Mary, who died in 1900, spent a lifetime at such work. In his autobiography, George wrote, "I had seen the tallow candle in my own home followed by the coal-oil lamp. I knew what it was to take care of the farm chores by the flickering, undependable light of the lantern in the mud and cold rains of the fall and the snow and icy winds of winter."

He also remembered his days as a Nebraska judge. His rulings saved hundreds of farmers, struggling through drought years, from foreclosures. Justice had to be just. And so did laws.

George was 75 years old when the REA started. He was one of the oldest members of Congress. He looked back at those years – especially recent years – with great satisfaction. He had served the voters well. But he had also served his conscience.

Sometimes he felt battle weary. Why had he fought so hard for laws he believed in? In years to come, few people would remember his name. Even fewer would know the struggle necessary to pass a single piece of his legislation. George remembered

The TVA helped employ workers unemployed after the Great Depression. The workers shown here helped build the Norris Dam. In October 1933, construction began on Norris Dam, located on the Clinch River, a tributary of the Tennessee River. It was completed in 1936.

By June, 1934, 9,173 people were working for the TVA. George lived to see 16 dams built by the TVA.

---

his brother, John Henry and his school friend, P.P. Hardy. Why had George fought so hard? Because it was the honorable thing to do.

George was a public servant. His job was to serve the people – all of the people. He once said, "I would rather go down to my political grave with a clear conscience than ride in the chariot of victory as a Congressional stool pigeon, the slave, the servant, or the vassal of any man."

❈ 24 ❈

One House, Undivided

During the elections of 1934, George decided not to campaign for any candidate – neither Republican nor Democrat. Instead he campaigned for another amendment. This time it was an amendment to the Nebraska constitution providing for a one-house legislature – called a unicameral legislature.

Nebraska, like other states, patterned its state government on the federal government. An executive branch (the governor), a judicial branch (the courts) and a legislative branch with two law-making houses.

Two-house legislatures hadn't always existed. Many states, including some of the original 13 colonies, used a unicameral – one house – legislature. After the federal constitution was ratified in 1789, however, all states adopted the two-house legislature.

George wanted Nebraska to adopt the one-house system. State government wasn't as complex as national government. Consequently, George felt a two-house legislature was illogical and clumsy. It was also expensive – requiring almost twice as much as a single house.

Many unicameral supporters favored continuing the tradition of political parties. But George, who had lost faith with partisan politics, wanted candidates for Nebraska's one-house legislature to run on a nonpartisan ballot. Candidates would campaign simply on their individual ideas – not on any party platform.

George's idea was adopted. Despite opposition from powerful leaders, including the *Omaha World-Herald*, Nebraskans voted for the unicameral legislature: 286,086 to 193,152. Nebraska became the only state in the country to have such a non-partisan, streamlined form of government.

TVA, REA, Yellow Dog Contract Act, Lame Duck Amendment, Unicameral Legislature – George had helped change the social, political and environmental fabric of the nation.

In 1936 when his term as Senator was over, he decided to run again. Not as a Republican. Not as a Democrat. Instead he ran as an Independent. Without the power and prestige of an official political party, many people said George was writing his political death notice.

But Nebraska voters thought otherwise. He was elected by a margin of almost 35,000 votes.

❦ 25 ❦

World War Again

In 1936, George Norris was seventy-five years
old. Many older politicians remained frozen in
the ideas of their youth, but George continued to
accept fresh ideas. Pres. Roosevelt's New Deal
represented many of George's dreams for helping
people. He once said that the government's job is to
protect and insure the well-being and happiness of
its citizens.

George never wavered from that goal. He realized, however, that the means for achieving his
goals altered according to the circumstances of the
times. He was willing to change with the times.
That willingness became especially important during George's next term in the Senate as an Independent.

Europe was at war. The trouble had started
when Germany began to take over neighboring
countries, first Austria and then part of Czechoslo-

101

vakia. The German dictator, Adolf Hitler, formed an alliance with Italy's dictator, Benito Mussolini. They called themselves the Axis Powers and together they planned to rule Europe. In response to these threats, Great Britain, France and the Soviet Union declared war against the invaders.

On the other side of the world, Japan invaded China. The military leaders in Japan planned to continue to expand into other territories in the Pacific region.

The U.S. tried to stay out of the conflicts. During World War I, George was an isolationist. But when he learned of the unspeakable horrors inflicted on people by the Axis Powers, he felt a moral obligation to help. George changed his views. How could a free nation such as America stand by and watch innocent people slaughtered?

Some leaders tried to stop the U.S. from joining the war. But on December 7, 1941, the Japanese bombed an American military base at Pearl Harbor in Hawaii. Eighteen U.S. warships were sunk or badly damaged, most of the airplanes on the ground were destroyed, nearly 2,500 soldiers, sailors and civilians were killed.

The next day Pres. Roosevelt addressed Congress. He called the attack "a date which will live in infamy." That same day Congress declared war against Japan. Three days later, the U.S. also declared war against the Axis Powers.

During the following years, George steadfastly supported the war effort. He was proud that the

TVA dams kept electricity running in the factories that supplied the U.S. military with weapons and equipment.

During the war, George worked on a bill to end poll taxes, a fee for voting. George knew why the taxes existed. The reason was racial. Popular among southern states, the taxes were set just high enough to keep poor black people from voting.

George said that the U.S. Constitution gave no state "the right to say that no one should be entitled to voted unless, for instance, he had red hair, or had attained the age of 100 years, or any other artificial qualification which, in fact, had nothing to do with the capacity of or real qualification of the voter.... Can it be said in view of the civilization of the present day that a man's poverty has anything to do with his qualification to vote?"

George was outraged that the country would ask poor young men and women to fight, and perhaps

In 1932, George, on the left, campaigned for Franklin Delano Roosevelt, second from right. Pres. Roosevelt said Norris was "one of the major prophets of America...the very perfect, gentle knight of American progressive ideals."

---

die, for their country in Europe and Japan, but would deny them the right to vote at home.

George fought against the poll tax for several years. But when Congress voted in 1942, during George's next Senate campaign, the bill failed to pass.

The defeat was hard. It was especially difficult because George knew he'd never have the chance to fight for it, or any other bill, in Congress again.

George wasn't returning to Washington, D.C. He lost the 1942 election.

26

The Fighter Comes Home

The campaign tired George out. But the defeat depressed him. George told reporters, who crowded around him afterwards, "The election is the most discouraging thing in my life."

He wrote to a friend, "Nebraska was tired of me."

Within days of arriving back home in McCook, however, George discovered the benefits of retirement. He had more time to spend with Ellie and his daughters. He had time to visit with his grandchildren.

Many of his friends back in Washington, D.C. offered him jobs, but George preferred to stay home, relax and work on his autobiography, which he called *Fighting Liberal*. Even Pres. Roosevelt wanted George's help. "I find myself sorely in need of you," Roosevelt wrote him.

On August 28, 1944, shortly after he finished

Sen. George Norris at his home office in McCook, Nebraska, after his retirement.

writing his autobiography, George suffered a stroke that left him paralyzed. A few days later he died.

George didn't live to see the U.S. and its allies win the war, although he never doubted that victory would come. He didn't live to see that in 1964 the 24th Amendment, outlawing poll taxes, was passed.

When George was a boy, he found his mother planting a tiny fruit tree. Sweat ran down her face and mud clung to her hands and knees. She was exhausted after working all day. George asked her why she bothered planting a tree she'd never live to see bearing fruit.

"I may never see this tree in bearing," she had said, "but somebody will."

George had learned that lesson well. He grew up to become one of the 20th century's finest Senators. Like all great leaders, he spent his life fighting for a future he would never see.

Christine Pappas is a life-long resident of Nebraska. She is currently pursuing her Ph.D. in political science at the University of Nebraska. She is the founding editor of "Plains Song Review," a literary magazine, and is the editor of "The Collected Short Stories of Dorothy Thomas," to be published by the University of Nebraska Press. *Fighting Statesman: Sen. George Norris* is her first children's book.

J.L. Wilkerson, a native of Kentucky, now lives in Kansas City, Missouri. A former teacher, Wilkerson has worked as a writer and editor for more than 25 years. She is an award-winning writer whose essays and articles have appeared in professional journals and popular magazines in the United States and Great Britain. She is the author of several regional history books. Wilkerson also has written children's books, including other biographies for Acorn Books' The Great Heartlanders Series.

Information about George Norris's life and times is available through these resources:
Fighting Liberal, by George W. Norris.
Integrity: The Life of George W. Norris, by Richard L. Neuberger and Stephen B. Kahn.
George W. Norris: The Making of a Progressive, 1861-1912, by Richard Lowitt.
George W. Norris: The Persistence of a Progressive, 1913-1933, by Richard Lowitt.
Profiles in Courage, by John F. Kennedy.
The George W. Norris Home and Museum, McCook, Nebraska.
These and other sources were used during the research of *Fighting Statesman: Sen. George Norris*.

ACORN BOOKS
THE GREAT HEARTLANDERS SERIES

Making history an active part of children's li
You can find this book and other Great Heartlanders boo
at your local fine bookstores.

For information about school rates for books and educational materials in THE GREAT HEARTLANDERS SERIES, contact

Acorn Books
THE GREAT HEARTLANDERS SERIES
7337 Terrace
Kansas City, MO 64114-1256

Other biographies in the series include:
Scribe of the Great Plains: Mari Sandoz
Champion of Arbor Day: J. Sterling Morton
A Doctor to Her People: Dr. Susan LaFlesche Picotte
From Slave To World-Class Horseman: Tom Bass
Frontier Freighter: Alexander Majors
American Illustrator: Rose O'Neill
Fighting Statesman: Sen. George Norris
Sad-Faced Clown: Emmett Kelly

Additional educational materials in THE GREAT
HEARTLANDERS SERIES are

- ♦ Activities Books   ♦ Celebration Kits
- ♦ Maps   ♦ "Factoid" Bookmarks
- ♦ Posters

To receive a free Great Heartlanders catalog and a complete list of series books and educational materials, write or
call Acorn Books.

Toll Free: 1-888-422-0320+READ (7323)
www.acornbks.com